THE GUIDE TO
AMERICAN
★ MONEY FOLDS ★

JODI FUKUMOTO

ISLAND HERITAGE™
PUBLISHING

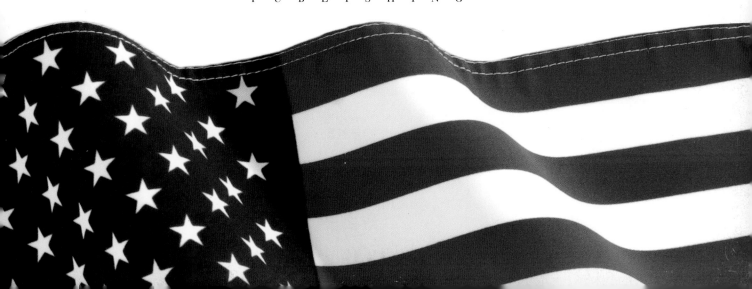

Dedication

This book is dedicated to my daughter,
Kiara Akemi

Acknowledgments

I would like to thank my mother, Barbara Fukumoto, and daughter, Kiara,
for their support and the others who have helped along the way.

ISLAND HERITAGE™
P U B L I S H I N G
A DIVISION OF THE MADDEN CORPORATION

94-411 KŌ'AKI STREET, WAIPAHU, HAWAI'I 96797
Orders: (800) 468-2800 • Information: (808) 564-8800
Fax: (808) 564-8877
islandheritage.com

ISBN: 0-93154-870-5
First Edition, Second Printing, 2006

Table of Contents

Money Folds

Introduction

Money folding is a pastime that symbolizes America's fun-loving spirit. Money folding allows us to poke a little fun at the almighty dollar and lets us turn convention into wonder and delight. It's both curious and amusing to discover the solemn portrait of our first president on the back of a Shirt—or to see our dollar presented in the unlikely forms of a Teddy Bear or a High-heel Shoe. Money folding permits us to take money out of context and assign it a priceless meaning. In tribute to America's sense of humor and, thankfully, her freedom of expression, this book presents a couple of American icons—the Eagle and the Statue of Liberty.

Money folds make imaginative and memorable presents. They add the element of surprise to an ordinary and usually anticipated monetary gift. The concept of using money folds as gifts is woven throughout this book. Most important is the variety of wonderful designs that can be used as gifts, including holiday motifs, American icons, and popular collectibles. To enhance gift giving, two box designs for presenting certain models are provided. A great gift idea (also mentioned later but worth mentioning twice) is to make your money fold out of a dollar rather than a larger denomination that will need to be unfolded to be spent. The money fold then becomes a treasured addition to your monetary gift.

Most model designs are appropriate for various different occasions. There are a few designs that have meanings and uses of which you may not be aware:

- The Pineapple, which is the international symbol of hospitality, can be used for housewarmings or as a token of appreciation whenever hospitality is extended.

- The Turtle, which represents long life in several cultures, can be presented as a birthday gift or as a lucky charm.

- The Lucky Frog, which has an open mouth in which to receive fortune, is a Japanese lucky charm. This charm must be received as a gift to be considered lucky. It is based on the belief that whatever is given will return tenfold. Use the Lucky Frog to bestow luck upon Las Vegas or Atlantic City vacationers or to anyone who makes investments. The frog design also makes a great gift for children because of its cavernous mouth in which to place coins, notes, or small gifts.

The Guide to American Money Folds uses a system of color to highlight the instructional arrows and lines in the diagrams, and to correlate them with the written instructions of folds that are more complex. These instructions, which can seem unnecessary or lengthy to the experienced folder, are written for the beginner. This concession is made because it is well known that experienced folders don't usually bother to read instructions anyway. So, at the very least, whether you're an enthusiast or a novice, please read Color Coding to learn the system of applied colors. Another concession made for the beginner is the added steps to a model's instructions. This is to not only insure that the instructions are understood but also to make it easier to accurately accomplish the required fold.

The Guide to American Money Folds is my fifth published origami book. *The Guide to American Money Folds* is a national version of *The Guide to Hawaiian-Style Money Folds*, from which some of the models were taken. The instructions were revised and a few of the models were renamed. My first four origami books, which have a Hawaiian theme, are sold primarily in Hawai'i stores but are also available on the Internet. They include:

The Guide to Hawaiian-Style Origami
The Guide to Hawaiian-Style Origami for Keiki (Children)
The Guide to Hawaiian-Style Money Folds
The Guide to Hawaiian-Style Origami Charms

Part One: How to Use This Book

SUPPLIES

Presenting Money

★ The Right Bill

Before selecting a bill to use for a particular model, study the folded examples and read the information that heads the model's instructions. It offers suggestions on which bills to use. Overall, the back of the one-dollar bill is favored—it is a practical choice that provides good color and design to most models.

As you know, bills of higher denominations bear several designs. In this book, the designs are labeled either *old* or *current*. Bills with the old designs are very ornate and, like the dollar, make wonderful models. Sadly, these bills are being withdrawn from circulation and are increasingly difficult to find, especially in good condition. Examples of models folded from these bills are still included for reference. Bills with the current designs are somewhat plain and often produce less impressive models. These bills are in the process of being reintroduced with a few design changes and a wash of colors. The colors, although subtle, definitely add to the appeal of certain models. (At the time of this writing, only the new twenty-dollar bill has been placed into circulation. Therefore, only the new twenty is seen in the examples of the models folded from current bills.)

Use a new, clean, and crisp bill. It not only makes a nicer model and gift, it is easier to crease and will hold a fold better than a used bill. A used bill will stretch when creases are set. Used bills also tend to absorb humidity, which loosens the folds of your model. Iron less-than-new bills to erase crinkles or even creases, and to remove moisture. Use medium heat.

As a gift idea, rather than fold a large-denomination bill that must be unfolded to be spent, add to your monetary gift a model folded from a one-dollar bill that can be saved as a keepsake.

★ Government Property

Please remember that all United States currency, even that in your possession, is government property. It is not against the law to fold money. However, it is against the law to intentionally destroy such property by gluing, cutting, or tearing it in any manner.

★ Foreign Currency

The money folds in this book are designed for U.S. currency. The proportions (ratio of width to length) of the models are based on the proportions of the dollar. Check Paper Substitutions for a list of acceptable sizes. The amount of leeway you are allowed on the provided dimensions or whether an unrelated size can be used is unknown. Keep in mind that an unspecified dimension may work for one model but not for another.

★ Descriptions

The *front* of a bill is the side with the portrait. As you'll notice in the diagrams, the front and back of the bill are displayed in two different colors. The layers of a model may display different shades of either color.

The *border* of a bill is the unprinted outer part of a bill. It is wider on the back of the bill than on the front. The different sections of the border may be uneven in width. Be sure to check the individual model information to see if your selected model requires a bill with specific border widths. Borders, as well as numerals, are only depicted when they pertain to the design or are necessary to the instructions.

The *border line* is the inside "edge" of the border. It is the line where the printed design of the bill begins.

Always start with the bill positioned upright (not upside down), unless otherwise directed.

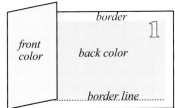

Model Care

To insure that your model/gift doesn't unfold:
• After or even during folding, iron your model on medium heat to set folds.
• Place a piece of double-stick tape between layers that tend to separate. *Do not use glue.*
• Use paper clips to hold and continue to set certain folds when storing your model.
• Store models in airtight containers or plastic bags.
• Store two-dimensional models between the pages of a heavy book.

Other Supplies

Each model lists required items in the section that introduces it. In general, in addition to cash, have on hand:

• Tweezers (to make and set small folds)
• Paper clips (to temporarily hold and set folds, or to hold folds during storage)
• Small bulldog clips (to use as clamps to set folds quickly, and for a stronger hold)
• Quality toothpicks, preferably round (to separate layers, and to help make or shape folds)
• Pencil or pen (to curl and round sections)
• Double-stick tape (to hold layers together)
• Scotch tape (for the Rose only)
• Origami paper, approximately 6 inches square (for boxes only)

If using paper instead of money, you will also need a ruler and a pair of scissors to measure and cut your paper to proper dimensions.

Paper Substitutions

Note: If you want to avoid the hows and whys, calculated paper sizes are offered below in red. Do not round off these figures but use them as they are.

To use paper in place of money and achieve the proper result, your paper must be either the same size as a dollar, which is approximately 2 5/8 inches by 6 1/8 inches, or it must have the same ratio of width to length as a dollar. The width-to-length ratio can be calculated as .75 : 1.75, and then can be expanded by multiplying both numbers by the same number:

$$(N = number)$$
$$.75 \times N : 1.75 \times N$$

This equation provides the following paper sizes (in any unit of measurement), or can be used to calculate any size needed:

1 1/2 x 3 1/2
2 1/4 x 5 1/4
3 x 7
3 3/4 x 8 3/4
4 1/2 x 10 1/2
5 1/4 x 12 1/4
6 x 14

If using a standard paper size, such as 8 1/2 inches by 11 inches (letter) or 6 inches square (origami), use one side as an established length and calculate the unknown width by dividing the length by 2.33.

$$length / 2.33 = width$$

Round off your result to the nearest 1/8. Calculated sizes using the lengths mentioned are:

2 1/2 x 6
3 5/8 x 8 1/2
4 3/4 x 11

Important:

- Before you cut paper for a particular model, read the information that precedes a model's instructions. It will note whether the model requires paper with sides that are the same, or similar, in color. Several money models display both sides of the paper, which may not be evident in the examples.

- In the instructions of several models, a fold is called for on the border line of the bill. When substituting paper that is not equal in size to the dollar, you will need to fold a section proportionate to that shown. If your paper is the same size as the dollar, you can fold a section the same width as a bill's border (approximately 1/4 inch).

THE FUNDAMENTALS OF ORIGAMI

★ Steps

- Steps are numbered. Follow the instructions step-by-step. Do not skip any steps.
- Each step contains a diagram and written instructions that show and tell you what to do. To help understand an instruction, look at the next step to see the result.
- An intermediate step may also follow an instruction to show how to accomplish the required fold. An intermediate step is labeled with a number and a lowercase letter.

★ Drawings

- The front and back sides of the bill or paper are depicted as two different colors.
- Instructional drawings do not always depict edges and folds perfectly aligned as they actually should be. This is in order to show existing folds and layers. In the example given, the left side is properly aligned while the right side is shown askew, exhibiting folds and layers.
- Drawings may be enlarged to clarify instructions. Significant enlargements are noted by the letter *E*.
- When a section of a drawing is outlined with a box, only that section is magnified and shown in the following steps.

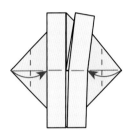

Align center lines to fold accurately.

★ Precision

- Take your time and be as precise as possible. Press hard to make sharp creases.
- Match and fold all pertinent edges, creases, and points exactly together.
- Align center lines when they pertain to a fold. A center line is a crease that runs through the center of your paper, model, or a section thereof. (See example above.)

THE KEY TO LINES, FOLDS, AND ARROWS

★ **Lines**

——————————— **Edge**

— — — — — — — **Fold**
(valley fold)

——————— **Crease**

—·—·—·—·—·—· **Mtn. Fold**
(mountain fold)

·· **Unseen Edge / Unseen Fold / Guide**

Edge lines and crease lines, which are usually **black,** are occasionally highlighted with color.
The color of all other lines may vary between red, blue, and **black.**

★ **Simple Folds and Arrows**

Arrows vary in color and size. Fold arrows also greatly vary in shape.

Fold
Fold section in front.

Unfold
Unfold section.

Fold; unfold
Make a crease.

 **Mtn. fold**
(mountain fold)
Fold section behind.

To mtn. fold:
Turn paper over.

Fold edge
to crease.

Turn paper
back over.

Lift
Lift flap
perpendicular.

To lift:
Fold to establish
crease if needed,
then lift flap at
right angle.

Indicates an important
edge, crease, or point (pt.)

Open layers, sides, or
model **here**

◯ **Press or pinch here**

▷ **Push here or push in**

  Turn paper / model over in direction of arrow

 Fold in-between layers
(see inside reverse fold)

★ Combination Folds

A combination fold combines two or more folds into a single step. These folds are made in a specific order, referred to as a folding procedure. In this book, the colors of the arrows and lines help determine the order of the required folds: *red* before *blue*, *blue* before ***black***. A folding procedure is listed for most combination folds, as they:are applied in the model instructions.

The standard combination folds used in this book are the inside reverse fold, outside reverse fold, squash fold, rabbit ear fold, and pleat fold. The folding procedure listed for a standard combination fold is not always the same. Sometimes the creases that make up a combination fold already exist. Other times, usually depending on the size of the fold, you are either directed to establish the required creases or you are given the option to do so. Beginners, please initially do so, it will help you understand how the fold is made and the actual placement of the creases.

The inside reverse fold, the most common combination fold, is explained here in greater detail to help you accomplish it accurately.

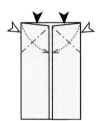

Example 1
Inside reverse fold each corner.
1. Establish optional creases by folding corner to center; unfold.
2. Open sides to symmetrically fold corner in.

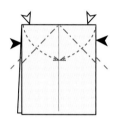

Example 2
Inside reverse fold corners:
1. Establish creases by evenly folding corners to center. Unfold.
2. Open sides to fold corners in on creases.

1. To establish creases, use inside reverse fold arrow ⌁⌁⌁➤ to show you where to fold an edge or pt. Align edges exactly and keep them aligned as you fold the corner(s) in as shown in the two examples below; unfold.

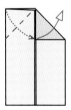

Example 1
To establish creases:
Fold corner to center as seen on right side of model. Unfold.
(It can be difficult to accurately crease two layers at once.
Minor adjustments can be easily made in the steps that follow.)

Example 2
To establish creases:
Fold corners to center as seen on right.
Push to stretch and align layers. Align flaps before setting both folds. Unfold.

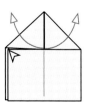

2. Open sides as indicated by arrow ◄. Push on edge indicated by arrow ◁ to fold corner to center on back crease.

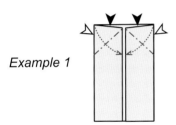

Example 1

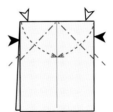

Example 2

3. Mtn. fold on remaining crease, redirecting it (changing its direction from a valley fold). To complete, fold new flap up (example 1) or side back over (example 2).

Example 1
Section of side edge is now a crease. Mtn. fold on crease, pinching sides together to create a flap. Make a precise pt. and match edges. Fold new flap up. Result is seen on right side.

Example 2
Push/fold section of top edge in to center. Mtn. fold on crease (diagram on left depicts crease on layer beneath). Fold side back over.

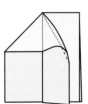

COLOR CODING

The colors red and blue are used to highlight instructional arrows and lines for the following purposes:

- To easily distinguish fold arrows and lines from edges and creases.

- To correlate the different arrows and lines of a diagram with the written instructions in folds that have more than one instructional arrow and/or line, such as the combination fold below. The colors also designate the order in which the folds are made. In general: red before blue; blue before **black.**

Rabbit ear fold.
1. Fold edges in on creases.
2. Fold sides together.
3. **Mtn. fold** is set by folding new flap down.

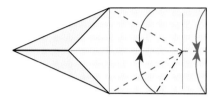

As seen, employing different colors makes it possible to easily explain combination folds in a model's instructions.

- To clearly define on a diagram unrelated instructions of a two-part step.
  As a rule, A is red and B is blue.

A 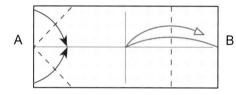 B

A. Fold edges to center.
B. Fold edge to crease; unfold.

For the few instructions with three parts, **black** is used as the third color.

- To identify notable edges and creases and to correlate them with the written instructions.

Fold midpoint down and edges to center.

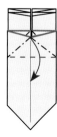

Money Folds

EAGLE

Eagle

To create the Eagle, use the front of any bill unless a green eagle is desired. The denomination of a bill is more evident in the final model when the front of the bill is used. Have on hand a pair of tweezers, a toothpick (preferably round), and a paper clip. Paper substitutions: The Eagle displays one side of the paper with the exception of the back of the eagle's head, which displays the other side.

1. Begin with the desired side up.
Fold in half; unfold.

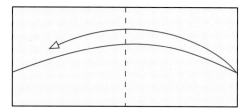

2. Evenly fold sides of edge to center; unfold.

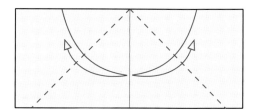

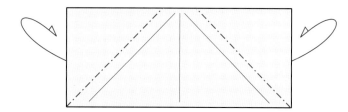

3. Mtn. fold edges behind to lower edge.

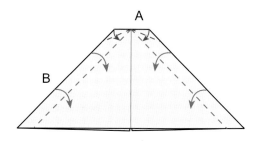

4.
A. Fold corners to creases.
B. Fold edges in on creases.
Keep bottom edges aligned.

5. Evenly fold sides of edge to center.

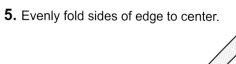

6. Turn model over.

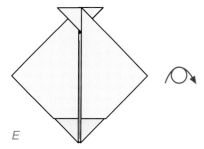

E

7. Fold pt. down to pt.

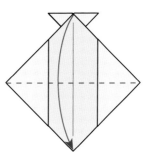

8. Align back flaps on center. Fold pt. up to intersection pt. of flaps.

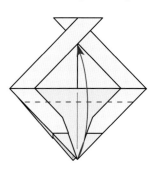

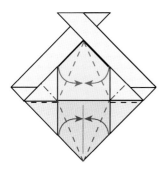

9. Rabbit ear fold both sides:
1. Fold edges to center. Do not fold flaps behind. Crease as shown. Unfold flaps out to sides.
2. Fold edges to center. Do not fold overlapping center layer behind.
3. Refold lower edges to center.
4. Set all folds.

10. Fold edges to center. Set folds only to pt. of layer beneath. Use paper clip to hold fold.

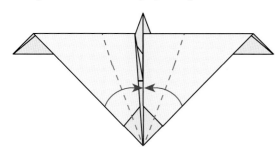

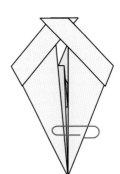

11. Turn model over.

Note: Use tweezers when needed to make or set smaller folds.

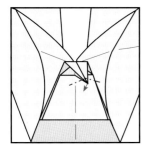

12.
A. Fold tip down. Make fold in line with edges behind.
B. Mtn. fold sides behind.
C. Fold tip up. *Note: Bottom tip section is slightly larger than top tip section.*

E

13.
A. Unfold edges of wings.
B. Unfold head flap.

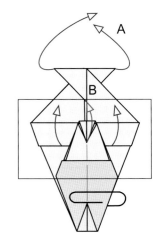

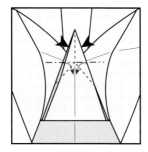

14. Rabbit ear fold top layer:
1. Use toothpick to separate layers.
2. Pinch fold sides of layer together.
3. Mtn. fold creases to center.

15. Pinch top layer of very tip of beak down. Fold tip down at right angle.

16.
A. Insert finger to open and round pockets. Shape wings as shown in result or as desired.
B. Remove paper clip. Use tweezers or round toothpick to curl flap down to create talons.

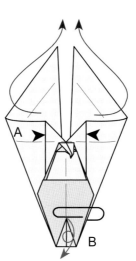

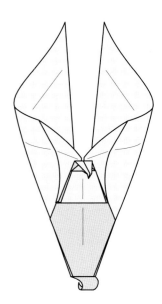

TRADITIONAL RING

Traditional Ring

See step 1 for a list of the most suitable bills, sides, and numerals. In general, use the side of any bill with a corner numeral that can be displayed within a 5/8-inch square. Try to select a bill with a right border (on the desired side) that is 1/4-inch wide or more. A bill with a left border of the required size is acceptable, but you will need to mirror the instructions from step 5 on. Instructions are given for bills with top and bottom borders of similar width. Have a toothpick on hand. Paper substitutions: The Traditional Ring displays one side of the paper.

5/8-inch square

1. Follow the specific instructions given for your selected bill and side. Begin with the desired side up.
Back of dollar (use upper numeral): Mtn. fold top edge behind on border line.
Front of dollar or current five (lower numeral): Mtn. fold top and bottom edges behind on border line.
Front of current ten, twenty, or fifty (lower right numeral): Mtn. fold bottom edge behind near or on border line.
Back of current fifty or hundred (upper numeral): Mtn. fold top and bottom edges behind on half border width.
Back of old bills (use any numeral of proper size): Mtn. fold edge nearest numeral behind on border line.

All bills: Proceed with the general instructions, which depict the back of the dollar only.

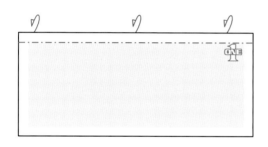

Turn model over this way.

OR

If chosen numeral is on bottom, **turn model over this way.**

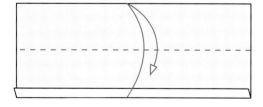

2. Fold edge to edge; unfold.

3. Fold edges to center.

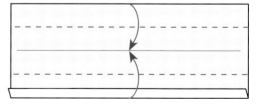

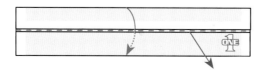

4. Lift bottom flap to fold top half tightly under. Match top edges.

Note: If numeral is upside down, rotate model to position shown.
To use numeral and border on left side, mirror instructions through step 10.

E

5.
A. Mtn. fold edge behind on border line OR farther in on other bills if needed to center numeral.
B. Mtn. fold section behind. Make distance of fold to edge same as width of strip, creating a square.

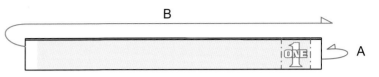

6. Round flap behind to desired ring size. Direct excess over square.

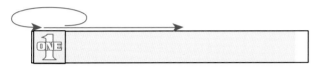

7. Fold edge of strip in line with edge of square beneath.

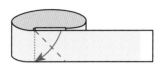

8. Lift square over top layers. Align edges as before. Unfold square flap.

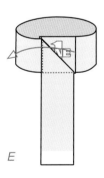

9. Tightly wrap/fold strip around band.

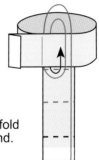

10. Fold square back over and tuck flap under all layers. Use a toothpick if needed.

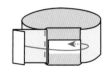

E

11. Fold edges in toward or to center.

E

TURTLE

Turtle

Use either side of any bill with an old design, including the dollar, or the back of any bill with a current design. Paper substitutions: The Turtle displays both sides of the paper. Paper with contrasting sides may work; see final diagram to determine if your selection is suitable.

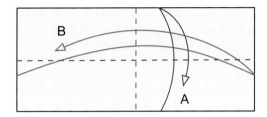

1. Begin with side intended as turtle's shell down.
A. Fold in half lengthwise; unfold.
B. Fold in half; unfold.

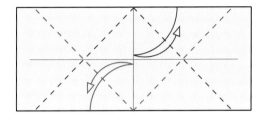

2. Evenly fold sides of edge to center line; unfold. Repeat.

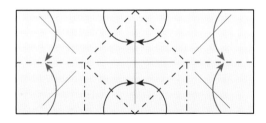

3. Rabbit ear fold each side:
1. Fold edges up as you fold sides together.
2. Fold new flap down. Flatten to set folds.

4. Squash fold flap:
1. Fold flap up. Lift perpendicular.
2. Open layers.
3. Flatten section on creases.

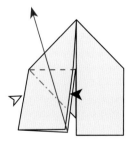

5. Fold flap over in line with edges beneath. Repeat steps 4 and 5 on right.

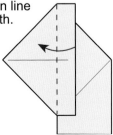

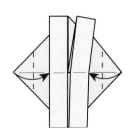

6. Fold corner pts. in.

Note: Check that back design is upright before proceeding.

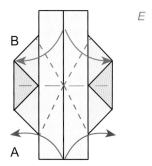

E

7.
A. Fold corner pts. up and out.
B. Fold edges to corner pts.

8. Fold corner pts. up.

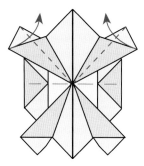

9. On each side:
A. Pinch tip. Lift edge to separate layers, unhooking fold from pleat beneath.
(See result on right.)
B. Hold layer down near center. Fold flap down on crease. Flatten.

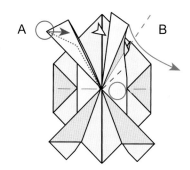

A

B

10. Fold sides together.

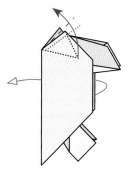

11. Inside reverse fold head:
1. Fold flap as shown; unfold.
2. Open sides to fold flap in on creases.

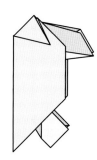

12. Reverse fold head out as you unfold back side almost completely. Pinch to define overlapping edges and folds.

Adjust flippers as desired.

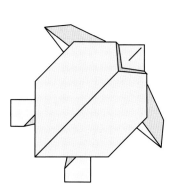

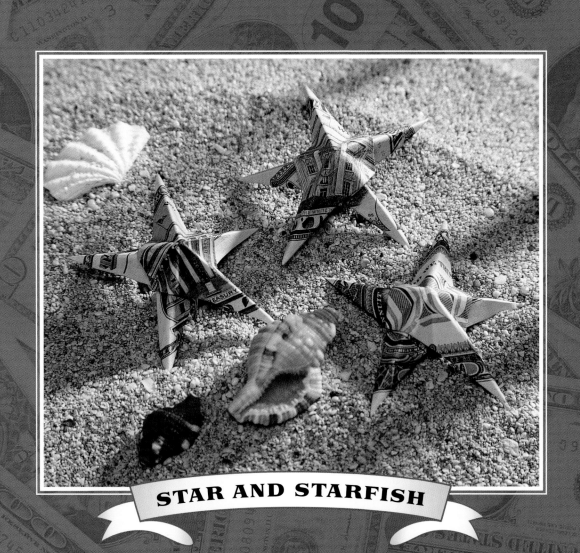

STAR AND STARFISH

Star and Starfish

Use the back of any bill. Ideally, select a bill with a thin right border. Use bulldog clips to set the final folds of the Starfish. Paper substitutions: Both models display one side of the paper on the front of the model.

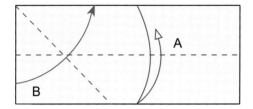

1. Begin with the desired side down.
A. Fold in half; unfold.
B. Fold edge to edge.

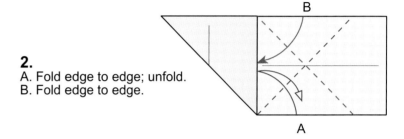

2.
A. Fold edge to edge; unfold.
B. Fold edge to edge.

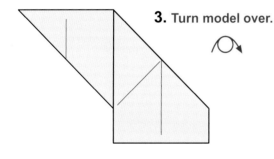

3. Turn model over.

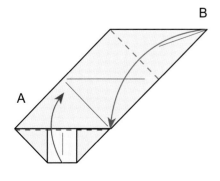

4.
A. Fold pt. in half up to crease behind. **Unfold.**
B. Fold corners of section in half.

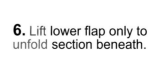

5.
A. Fold section up along edge.
B. Fold pt. to corner pt.

6. Lift lower flap only to unfold section beneath.

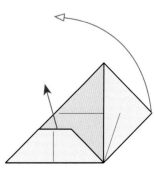

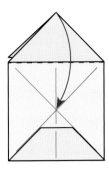

7. Fold section down tightly against edge. Do not cover diagonal creases. Adjust lower flap if necessary to show creases.

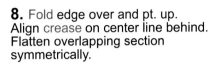

8. Fold edge over and pt. up. Align crease on center line behind. Flatten overlapping section symmetrically.

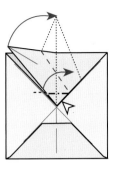

9. Fold sides in on creases. Align all edges. Set folds.

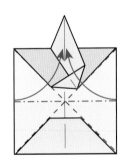

10. Pinch front flaps. Fold midpt. of edge to pt. Crease only on center.

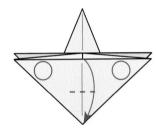

11. Note indicated pt. **Turn model over.**

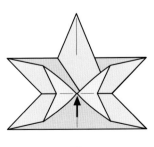

12. Pivot upper section on center pt. behind. Align edge of top flap with edge of lower flap. Bottom pt. of triangular section remains on edge.

13. Push to align layers if needed. **Turn model over.**

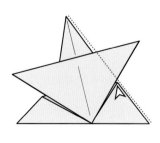

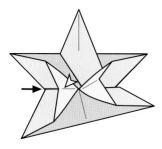

14. Set indicated fold. Flatten overlapping section symmetrically.

15.
A. Pleat fold:
1. Mtn. fold crease into edge.
2. Fold new edge over, aligning indicated edge with right edge of top flap.
B. Set fold beneath overlapping section. Flatten overlapping section symmetrically. **Turn model over.**

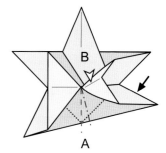

16. Make needed adjustments. Set all folds.

This is the completed Star.
Complete step 17 to create the Starfish.

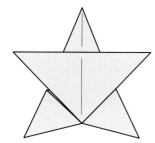

17. Turn model over.

In order shown, pinch fold sides of each arm together up to center pt. Work both front and back. As you proceed, fold together pairs of adjacent arms. Use bulldog clips to set final folds. Turn model back over. Partially open sides of arms and evenly arrange.

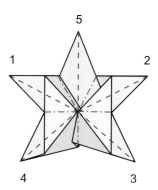

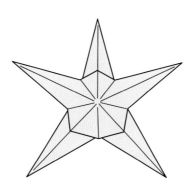

LUCKY FROG

Lucky Frog

For the greenest frog, use the back of a one-dollar bill. Have a toothpick on hand. Paper substitutions: The Lucky Frog displays both sides of the paper. Select paper with sides of the same or similar color.

1. Begin with the desired side of the bill or paper up.
Note: Position the desired design to be displayed on your frog's back on the left side. For instance, from the back of a dollar, place either the pyramid or United State's seal on the left. The bill may be upside down.

Fold in half; unfold.

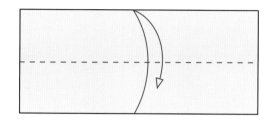

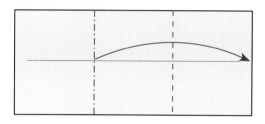

2. Fold into equal thirds:
1. Layer left over right without creasing. Create an *S* configuration with top edge. (See 2a.)
2. Adjust sections of edge into equal lengths.
3. Hold aligned edges in place. Set folds.

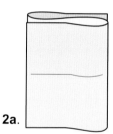

2a.

Rotate model as shown.
Note: Back design is up.

3.
A. Fold in half to redefine crease; unfold.
B. Evenly fold corners to center. Unfold.

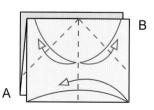

4. Squash fold flap:
1. Fold corner to corner.
2. Stretch and flatten section on creases.

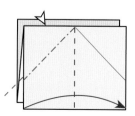

5. Fold edge to center.

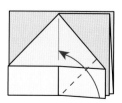

6. Fold flap back. Repeat steps 4 to 6 on right.

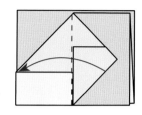

E

7. Turn model over.

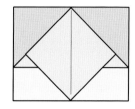

8. Fold sides in to center.

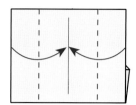

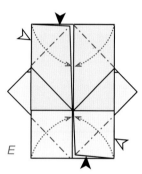

E

9. Inside reverse fold each corner:
1. Establish optional creases by folding corner to center; unfold.
2. Open sides to symmetrically fold corner in.

10. Pinch flaps. Pull them up and out to the sides, flattening center pt. Continue to pinch edges of each flap together up to center. Set all folds.

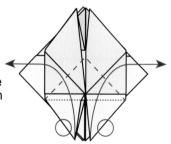

11.
A. Fold pt. to corner pt. on both sides.
B. Fold pt. up on border line behind.

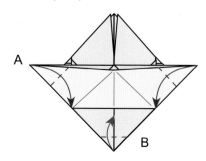

A

B

12. Fold flaps in half.

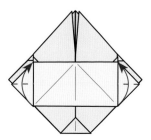

13. Fold legs in.

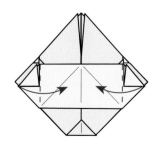

E

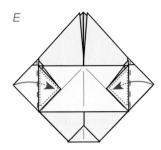

14. Fold side tabs into pockets hidden behind legs, locking back layers together.
Optional: Use toothpick to accomplish.

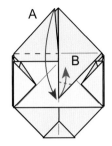

15. On each side:
A. Fold flap down as shown on right.
B. Fold tip of flap up on an angle.

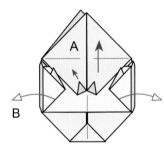

16.
A. Lift front feet then front legs perpendicular.
B. Partially unfold back legs, keeping them angled inward.

Turn model over.

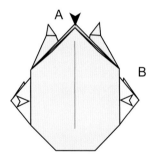

17.
A. Push on sides. Insert finger between layers to open mouth and to slightly round frog's back.
B. Place model on a flat surface. Adjust legs and feet until feet rest firmly on surface.

Insert a lucky penny or gold dollar in the mouth of your frog.

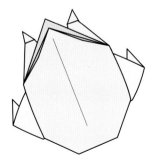

BUTTERFLY

Butterfly

All bills are suitable. Although the back of a bill with a current design (without added colors) will create a mainly white model. The Butterfly displays the complete numeral denomination of all bills except that on the front of the hundred. Select bills with even borders or, at the very least, even side borders. A toothpick and a bulldog clip are handy. Paper subsitutions: The front of the Butterfly, with the exception of its abdomen displays one side of the paper and the back, primarily the other side.

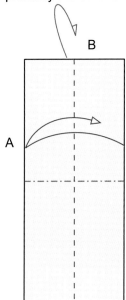

1. Begin with the desired side down.
A. Fold in half; unfold.
B. Mtn. fold in half.

2. Inside reverse fold corners:
1. Establish creases by evenly folding corners to center. (See 2a.) Unfold.
2. Open sides to fold corners in on creases.

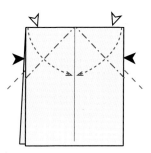

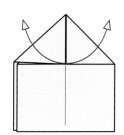

2a.

3. Fold section up along edges.
Mtn. fold section behind up.
Match sides. Unfold.

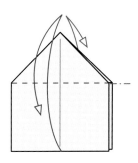

4. Fold edge to edge.
Mtn. fold edge behind to edge.

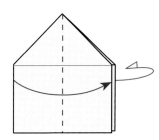

5. Fold edges to center.
Crease only as shown.
Unfold. Repeat behind.

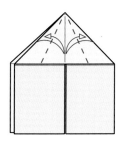

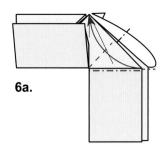

6a.

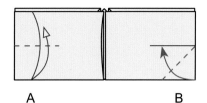

A   B

6. Fold corner pt. up to pt. Reestablish folds on both sides.
Fold corner pt. behind to pt. Repeat on opposite side. (See 6a.)

7. On each side:
A. Fold edge to edge.
Crease only as shown. Unfold.
B. Fold corner to crease. **Unfold.**

*Note: Place side intended as lower wings
on top. Design will be upside down.*

8. Open center flaps. Do not flatten.

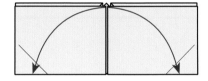

9. Rabbit ear fold each side:
1. Fold edges of flap together,
folding edges in on creases.
2. Fold flap up to set mtn.
fold. **Unfold.** (Do not flatten.)

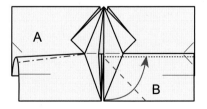

10. On each side:
A. Align overlapping side edges.
Flatten section as seen on right.
B. Fold corner up as shown or as desired.
Note: Fold determines shape of lower wing.

11. Fold pt. down in line with
edge. Fold edges in to center
and flatten.

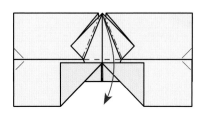

12. Turn model over.

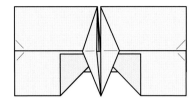

13.
A. Pinch as shown. Gently pull outer layers outward to reveal pt. Fold pt. up.
B. On each side:
Unfold overlap enough to inside reverse fold corner in on creases.

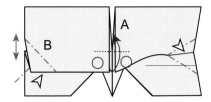

Step 14 offers two views. Both depict instructions on left and results on right. Written instructions refer to front view only.

14. On each side:
A. Inside reverse fold edges of inverted section together.
B. Mtn. fold corner behind to shape wing. Fold corner back up just past new edge to create antenna.

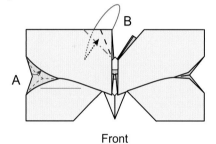

Front

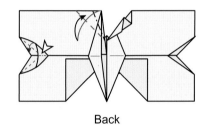

Back

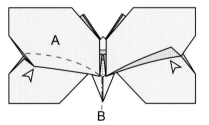

15.
A. On each side:
Fold overlapping edge up as seen on right. Push folded edge flat on outer half of wing.
B. Mtn. fold sides of lowest section together.
Optional: Use bulldog clip to temporarily set fold or to keep wings positioned back.

Pinch/release sides of abdomen to emulate the flutter of a butterfly's wings.

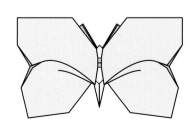

FLOWERS

Flowers

The instruction to Flowers covers both versions seen in the examples, "in bloom" (smaller flower) and "full bloom." To create either version, use the back of any bill. Have on hand a toothpick, a pair of tweezers, and preferably bulldog clips, though paper clips will suffice. Paper substitutions: Consider that the front of this model displays one side of the paper and the back displays both sides; select paper accordingly.

1. Begin with the desired side up.
Fold in half; unfold.

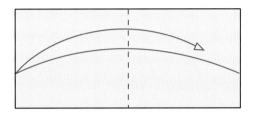

2. Fold edges to center.

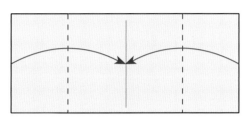

3. Fold sides of top layer in half.

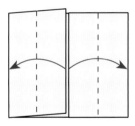

4. Turn model over to fold edges of sides to center line.

5. Fold corners of flaps to center. Repeat behind. Match folds.

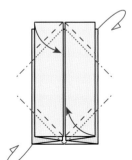

6.
A. Unfold all corners.
B. With single layer flaps on top, mtn. fold model in half.

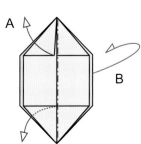

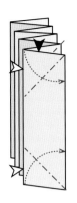

7. Open sides of flap to inside reverse fold both corners in on creases. Repeat on remaining flaps.

E

Rotate model as shown.
8. Fold outer flaps in half.

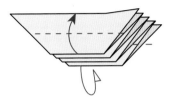

9. Fold flap up.

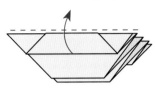

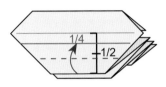

1/4

1/2

10. Fold edge to 1/4 distance from crease.
Note: Determine 1/2 distance first.

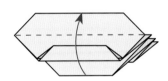

11. Fold two flaps up.

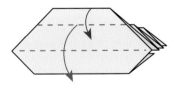

12. Fold edge down in line with edge behind. Fold new edge down on crease.

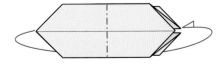

13. Mtn. fold in half. **Unfold.**

14. Fold sides together.

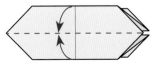

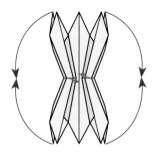

15. Fold sides together on creases to fan out petals. Use bulldog clips to hold sides together near center or use paper clips on end flaps. Slightly offset folds at center to accomplish fold.

16. Pinch edges between all petals to raise and set. **Turn model over.**

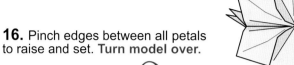

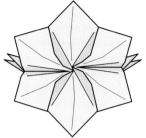

To complete variation "full bloom," proceed to step 17.
To create variation "in bloom," first complete steps in inset below.

16A. Use tweezers to offset folds at center about 1/4 inch. Pinch all folds together at center.

16B. Pinch both sides front and back on edges as shown. Raise sides as seen in front view to push corners through as indicated in back view, extending the bottom edge.

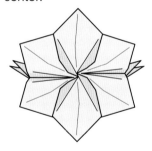

Front

Back

16C. Note same indicated corners. Pinch edges to set.
16D. On front of model: Pinch/raise edges between petals to reshape. **Turn model over.**

Proceed with general instructions, which depict variation "full bloom."

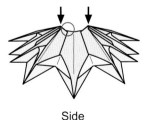

Side

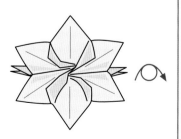

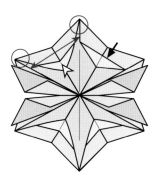

17. Pinch flaps of adjacent petals flat on center. Symmetrically stretch and flatten overlapping section as indicated on right. Repeat on all sections.

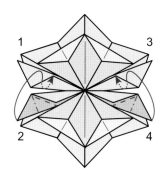

Complete steps 18 and 19 on left side first, then on right side using petals 3 and 4.

18. Pinch petals 1 and 2 together from beneath. Use a toothpick to fold flap (darker shade) between upper petal and center flap. Push on center of flap, folding it in half between layers.

19. Use a toothpick to fold flap in between lower petal and center flap. Push on middle of flap, folding it in half between layers.

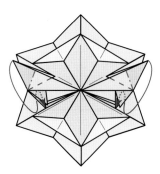

20. Turn model over.

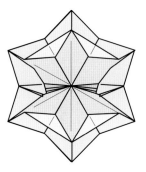

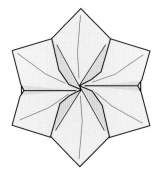

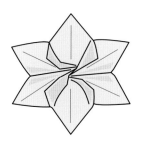

ANGEL

Angel

Use the front of a current five-dollar bill to create a mainly white model. Otherwise, use the back of a dollar. When possible, select a bill with top and bottom borders of similar width on both sides. Have a pair of tweezers and a toothpick handy. Paper substitutions: The Angel displays both sides of the paper.

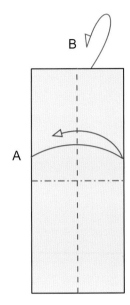

1. Begin with the desired side up and the top edge on right.
A. Fold in half; unfold.
B. Mtn. fold in half.

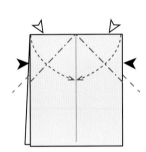

Note: Side intended as front of model is up.

2a.

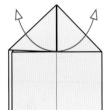

2. Inside reverse fold corners:
1. Establish creases by evenly folding corners to center. (See 2a.) Unfold.
2. Open sides to fold corners in on creases.

3. Fold flap up along edges beneath.

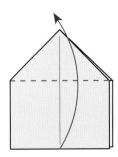

4. Fold flap down. Make fold 1/8-inch distance from edge on center.

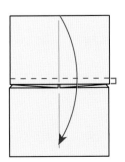

5. Fold pt. to 1/4-inch distance from edge.

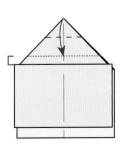

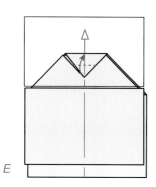

6. Fold pt. to edge. Crease well. Unfold flap completely.

E

7. Fold pt. down on same crease to redirect. **Unfold.**

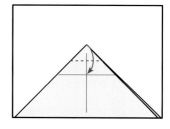

8. Flatten tip on creases:
1. Lift section perpendicular.
2. Stretch open sides. Flatten point on creases. (See 8a.)

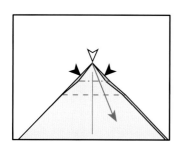

8a.

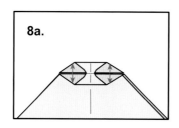

9. Fold edge up.

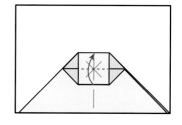

10. Fold each side in. Begin at top. Extend fold down to bottom corner.

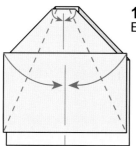

11. Fold front flap down.

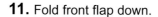

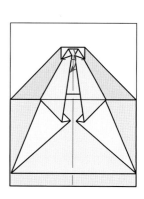

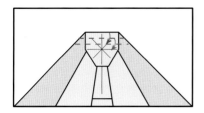

12. Fold edge 1/3 distance to crease. Fold new edge just below crease.

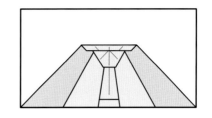

13. Turn model over.

14. Fold sides in to center.

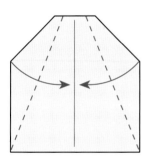

15. Fold flap up between pts.

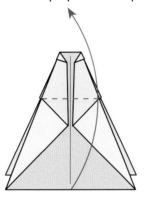

16. Fold flap down on *V* pt. behind. Do not set.

17. Fold model in half.

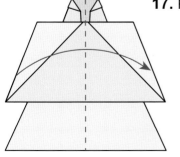

E

18. Pinch wings. Slightly pivot them up to extend indicated layers/hair on both sides. Pinch firmly to set new folds within. Pinch bottom of wings and slowly roll farther up.

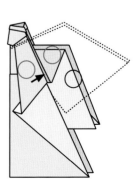

19.

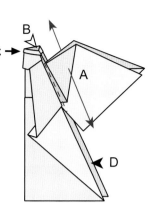

A. Outstretch wings to sides against back edges.
B. Use tweezers or toothpick to lift and round back layers of head.
C. Pinch top and bottom edges of halo with tweezers to compress, extending halo over face.
D. Open sides to stand model.

20.

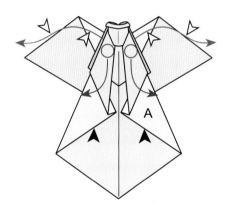

A. Lightly pinch model.
Open layers to lift arms and hands.
B. Pinch and shape edges of wings.

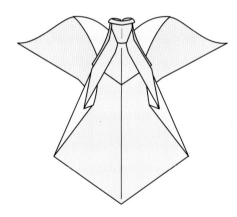

TEDDY BEAR

Teddy Bear

A one-dollar bill is required to fold the Teddy Bear, which ulitlizes the design on the back of the bill. Select a bill with even back borders. The top and bottom borders of the bill must be especially even in order for the bear's face to be centered. Have a pair of tweezers, a toothpick, and a pencil on hand. Paper substitutions: The Teddy Bear displays one side of the paper.

1. Place end intended as head on bottom and desired side down.
A. Fold in half; unfold.
B. Fold corner to edge; unfold.
Repeat.

2. Fold sides in on creases. Align all edges. Set folds.

Note: Use tweezers when needed to make and set smaller folds.

3. Inside reverse fold each tip:
1. Fold pt. of flap to border line as seen on left.
2. Open layers to fold tip in on creases.

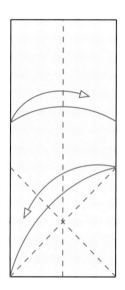

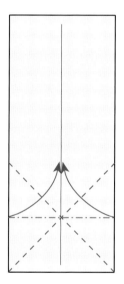

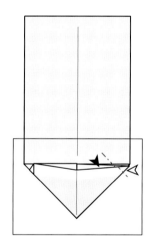

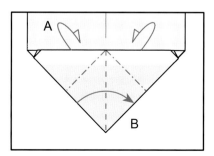

4.
A. Mtn. fold flaps in half.
B. Fold left flap to right.

5. Fold flap up at an angle. Align edge of flap on indicated border line. Repeat with other flap. Match folds.

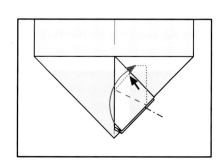

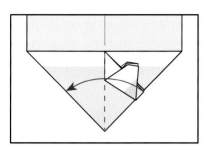

6. Fold open left side.
Adjust ears if desired.

7.
A. Mtn. fold corners behind.
B. Fold pt. up in line with
dots in eyes.

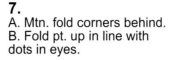
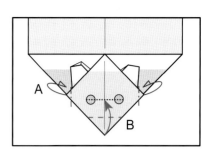

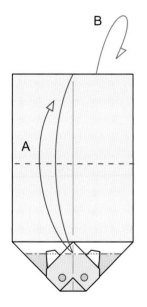

8.
A. Fold edge to
border line; unfold.
B. Mtn. fold section
behind on border line.
Do not fold ears.

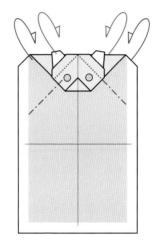

9. Turn model over.
Fold edges to center.

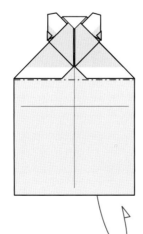

10. Mtn. fold
section behind.

11.
A. Mtn. fold edge on border line.
B. Mtn. fold section behind
on crease. Lift head over
new edge if needed.

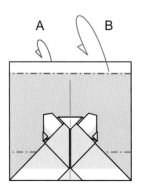

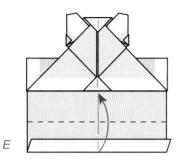

12. Fold edge to edge.

E

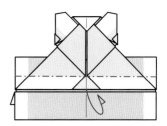

13. Mtn. fold section under on border line.

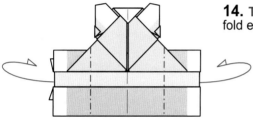

14. Turn model over and fold edges to center. **Unfold.**

Complete steps 15 and 16 on left side, then on right.

15. Fold edge of top layer in. Make fold only to pt. shown.

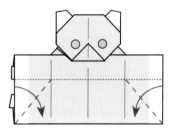

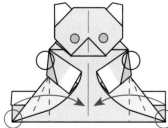

16. Pinch corner to hold last fold in place. Fold leg under corner of top leg and to center on crease. Fold is made in the process. Flatten top leg down. **Pinch** shoulder to set fold.

17.
A. Inside reverse fold each corner: open side to push/fold corner in.
B. Fold tip of nose down, then perpendicular.

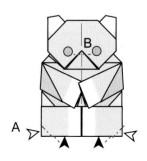

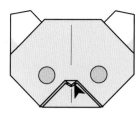 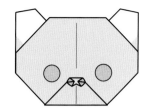

18. Use a toothpick to round open layers to form nostrils and to slightly flatten pt. of triangular section.

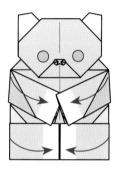

19. Wrap section of legs around a pencil to round them out.

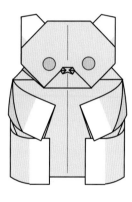

PINEAPPLE

Pineapple

Use the back of any bill. The twenty-dollar bill tinted with color especially creates an interesting model. Select a bill with a thin top border whenever possible. Paper substitutions: The Pineapple displays one side of the paper.

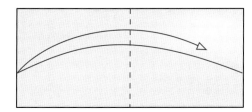

1. Begin with the desired side down.
Fold in half; unfold.

2. Evenly fold sides of edge to center.

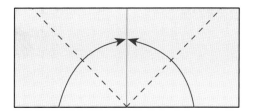

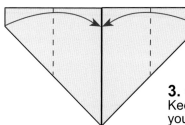

3. On each side:
Keep edge on center as
you fold side edge to center.

5. Unfold paper or bill
completely.

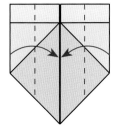

4. On each side:
Keep edges on center as
you fold side edge to center.

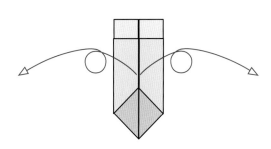

6.
A. Fold edges up on creases to redirect.
Mtn. fold creases. Crease only as shown.
Unfold.
B. Refold edges to center.

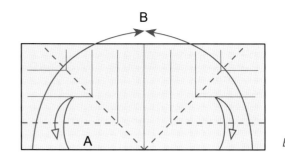

7. Open sides to inside reverse fold end in and through on creases.

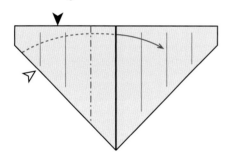

8. Open sides to inside reverse fold end back in and through on creases.

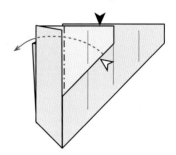

9. Repeat steps 7 and 8 on right side.

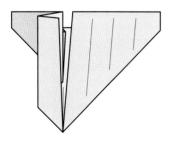

10. Turn model over.

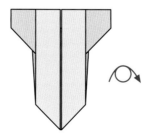

11. Fold edges to center.

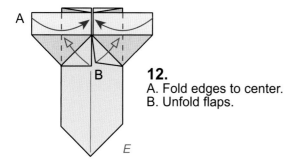

A

B

E

12.
A. Fold edges to center.
B. Unfold flaps.

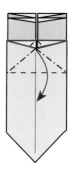

13. Fold midpt. down and edges to center on creases.

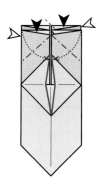

14. Inside reverse fold each corner:
1. Establish optional creases by folding corner of flap to center; unfold.
2. Open sides to symmetrically fold corner in.

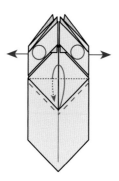

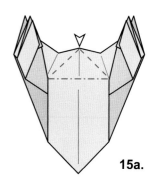

15a.

15. Pinch all flaps. Pull sides out and push midpt. down to refold pt. in on creases. (See 15a.)

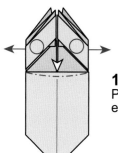

16. Pull sides out. Push to mtn. fold edge behind.

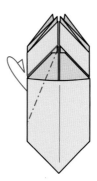

17. Mtn. fold pt. in half, aligning edge behind on center.
Turn model over to complete fold.
Fold in the two sets of layers separately.

Note: Outer layer determines shape of fruit and can be loosened later if needed to fan out crown.

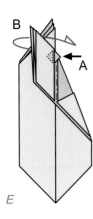

18.
A. Fold indicated tab in between layers.
B. Mtn. fold flaps through center. Wrap tightly around side.

Turn model over. Repeat steps 17 and 18 on left.

E

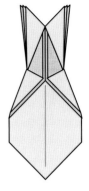

19. **Turn model over.**

20.
A. Mtn. fold tip behind on border line.
B. Lift flaps. *Optional: To hold sides of crown together, unfold small tab of 18A located behind. Fold between first two layers of the section on opposite side.* Fan out crown.

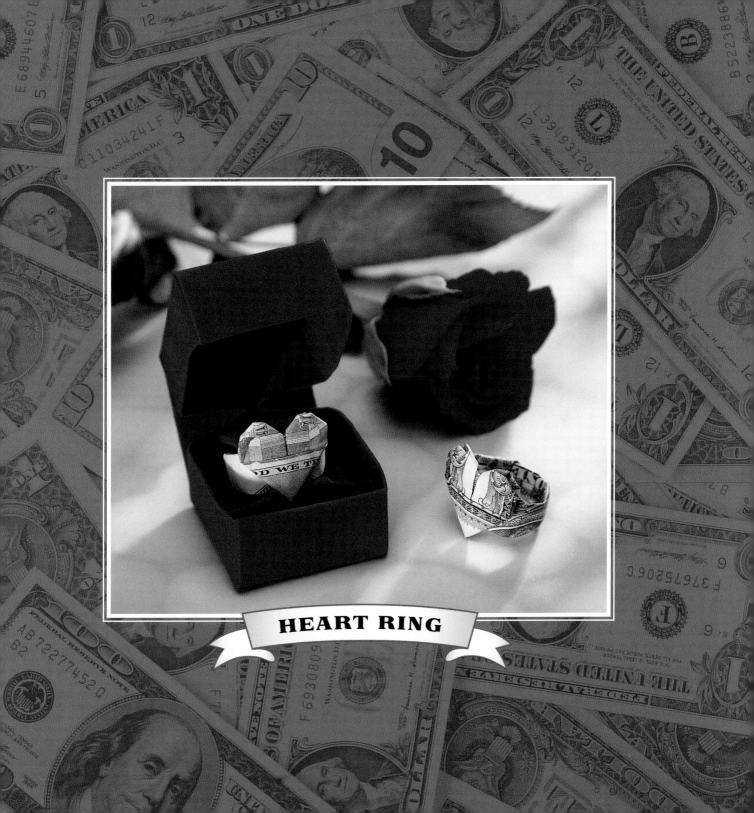

HEART RING

Heart Ring

Use the back of any bill. Note that the denomination of the bill is not displayed. You will need a pencil. A pair of tweezers is handy but optional. Paper substitutions: The Heart Ring displays one side of the paper.

1. Begin with the desired side down.
A. Fold in half; unfold.
B. Fold edge to crease.

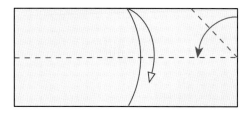

2. Fold each edge in 1/3 distance to center.

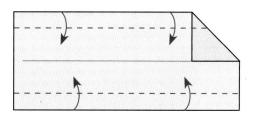

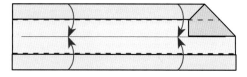

3. Fold edges to center.
Note: On each side, width of flaps equals remaining distance to center.

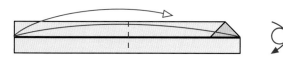

4. Fold in half; unfold. **Turn model over.**

5. Evenly fold sides of top edge to center. Crease as shown. **Unfold.** Evenly fold sides of bottom edge to center. Crease as shown.

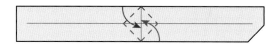

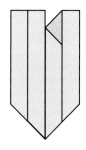

6. Turn model over.

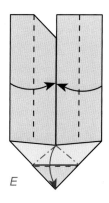

7. Fold midpt. of edge to pt. as you **fold** edges to center.

8. Insert flap within pocket beneath to lock sides together.

E

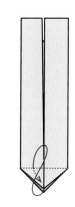

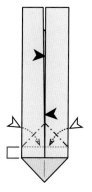

9. Inside reverse fold each flap 3/16 to 1/4 inch above corner pt. Open sides to symmetrically fold flap in and through.

Turn model over.

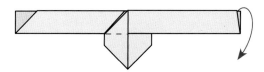

10. Fold side open.

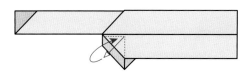

11. Lift side of flap and pull corner out. Refold corner over flap.

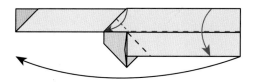

12. Fold pt. to pt. while folding sides together and folding flap to the left.

13. Unfold side.

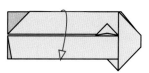

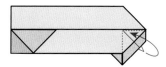

14. Lift side of flap and pull corner out. Refold corner over flap.

15. Fold pt. to pt. Fold sides together. Fold flap to the right.

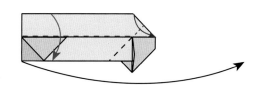

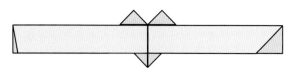

16. Turn model over.

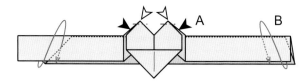

17.
A. Inside reverse fold each tip by opening side to push/fold tip in.
B. Lift flap beneath to fold top flap between layers on both sides.

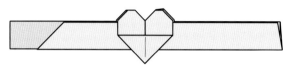

18. Turn model over.

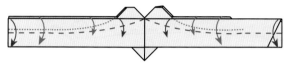

19. On each side:
Separately fold layers down. Fold end first. Slightly bend and round sides to make folds.

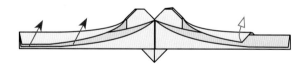

20. Use a pencil to further round sides and set folds. Lift both flaps on left. Unfold top flap on right.

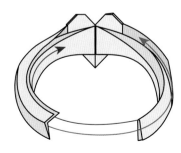

21. Round right side inside of left side. Slip lower edge of left side between layers of right side. Refold top edges in, left first. Mold and round sides.

FOUR-LEAF CLOVER

Four-leaf Clover

To create the "greenest" four-leaf clover, use the back of a one-dollar bill. A bill with even back borders is required. You will need a bulldog clip or a paper clip. Paper substitutions: The Four-leaf Clover displays one side of the paper on the front of the model, and both sides on the back .

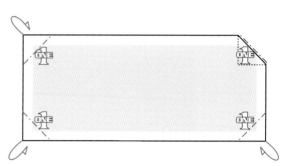

Note: Numerals are depicted only when they apply to instructions.

1. Begin with the desired side up.
Symmetrically mtn. fold top right corner behind as shown. Work front and back of bill to fold as close as possible to the word and numeral of the denomination.
Mtn. fold remaining corners to match initial fold.

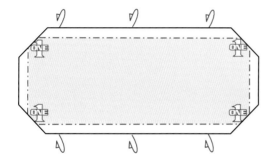

2. Mtn. fold edges behind on border lines.

3. Fold in half; unfold. **Turn model over.**

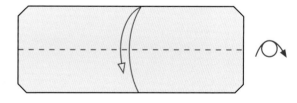

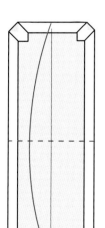

Rotate model as shown.
4. Fold in half.

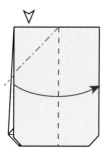

5. Squash fold flap:
1. Establish creases by evenly folding corner to center. (See 5a.) Unfold.
2. Fold edge to edge.
3. Stretch overlapping section and flatten on creases.

Repeat 2 and 3 behind.

5a.

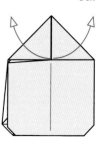

6. Fold edges to edge.
Turn model over.

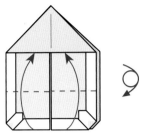

7.
A. Fold sides in keeping center edges aligned. Match folds.
B. Unfold flaps from behind.

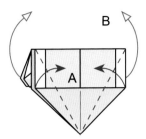

8. Mtn. fold sides behind, matching front folds.

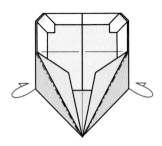

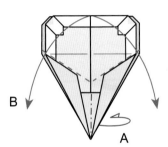

9.
A. Mtn. fold sides together.
B. Fold each flap down against edge. Align all edges. (See 9a.) Unfold flaps.

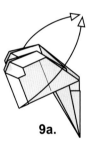

9a.

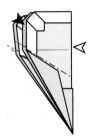

10. Open sides to inside reverse fold each flap in and through on creases shown.

Continue to align all folds through step 13.

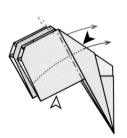

11a.

11. Inside reverse fold each flap:
1. Establish creases by folding flap up against edge. (See 11a.) Unfold.
2. Open layers to fold flap through on creases.

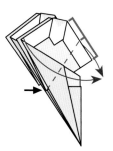 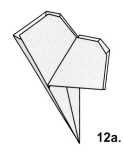

12a.

12. Fold outer flaps down between midpt. of edge and indicated *V* pt. (See 12a.) **Unfold** flaps and sides.

13. On each side:
Symmetrically fold corner down. Hold in place. Lift flap to release fold beneath. Refold flap back down, locking corner in place.

Turn model over and repeat. Match folds.

Note: Position side with creases up.

14. Inside reverse fold corner on each flap:
1. Establish creases by folding edge to crease. (See 14a.) Unfold.
2. Open layers to fold corner in on creases.

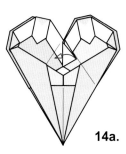

14a.

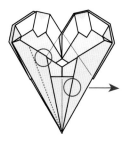

15. Lightly pinch left flap near top. Firmly pinch right side near center. Slowly pull right side away from left, extending center section enough to later fold left edge to center. (See step 16.) Set new folds on front and back.

Mirror procedure to extend center section on right side. (See 15a.)

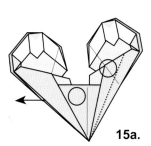

15a.

Note: Open sides to see if numeral on back flap is upright. If not, turn model over.

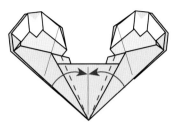

16. Fold edges to center.

17. Turn model over.

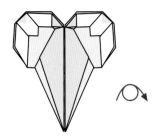

18. Fold all flaps down. Fold side with creases first. Fold other side to match.

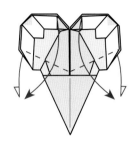

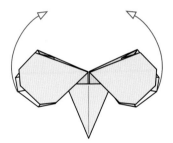

19. Unfold back flaps.

Note: Numerals are upright.

20. Pinch to hold leaves together. Pinch mtn. fold sides of stem together up to base of leaves. Bend and adjust sections of leaves into place. Use a clip to set stem fold. Curl stem.

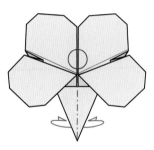

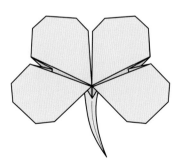

SHIRT

Shirt

Use a one-dollar bill to create a shirt with a lot of print and color. A shirt folded from a one (or any bill with an old design) will also have a portrait centered on the back. Select a bill with even back borders. Have on hand a toothpick. Paper substitutions: Select paper with sides of the same color.

1. Begin with the side intended as the shirt's front facing down.
Fold in half; unfold.

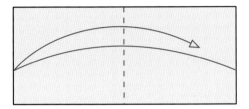

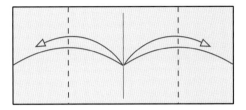

2. Fold edges to center; unfold.

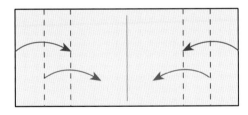

3. On each side:
Fold edge to crease.
Fold new edge in on crease.

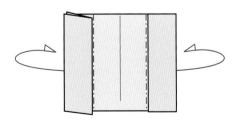

4. Mtn. fold edges behind to center.
Unfold completely.

Note: Side/design of shirt's back is up.

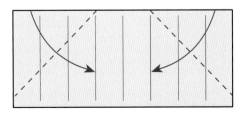

5. Fold sides of edge to creases.

6. On each side:
Pinch to keep edge of flap aligned on crease.
Mtn. fold edge behind to center.

Unfold completely.

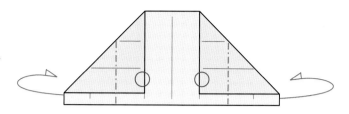

7. Rabbit ear fold both sides:
1. To begin, fold sides up on creases only.
Bend midsection of top edge up and later down.

Complete steps 7 and 8 on one side first, then the other.

2. Pinch/fold edges of corner together.
3. Fold sides in and completely down on creases only.
4. Fold new flap down. Do not set.

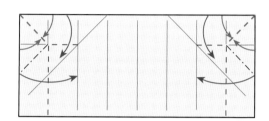

8. Align creases on top flap with edges beneath before setting all pertaining folds. Lift midsection of top edge.
Refold side in on creases, starting with diagonal.
Flatten to set folds.

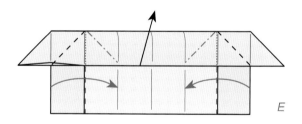

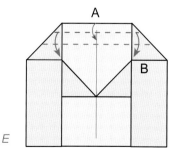

9.
A. Fold edge down slightly above border line behind.
Leave a narrow band of white border behind to highlight edge of collar.
B. Fold new edge to pt., slightly above shoulder line.

E

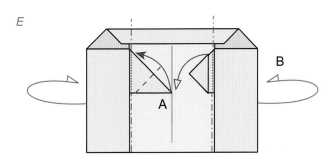

10.
A. Fold pt. of each sleeve up as seen on right; unfold.
B. Mtn. fold edges behind to center on creases.

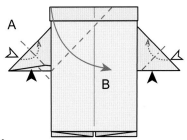

11.
A. Open sides of sleeves and inside reverse fold ends in on creases.
B. Fold corner down. Do not set fold.

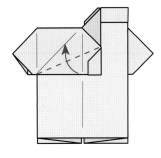

12. Fold aligned edges to crease.

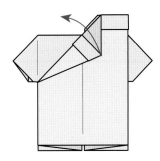

13. Fold flap back up. Repeat steps 11B to 13 on opposite side.

14. Turn model over.

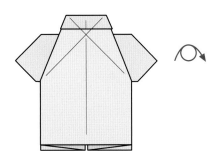

15. Realign sides if necessary. Open side to fold inside flap down. Repeat on right.

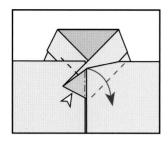

16. Fold corner down, parallel to collar's edge beneath. Slowly flatten overlapping section, creating a fold in line with edge beneath. Repeat on left.

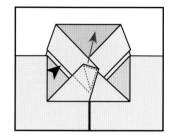

17. Lift hidden edge of collar. Gently stretch it and overlapping section up to create a square corner. Do not stretch overlapping section flat. Pinch flat instead. Pinch to set new fold.

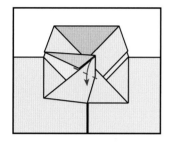

18. Fold edge of collar down. Repeat steps 17 and 18 on right.

19. On each side use a toothpick to:
1. Lift collar flap as you push down on inside of collar to splay flap over lapel.
2. Adjust lapel and shape collar if needed.

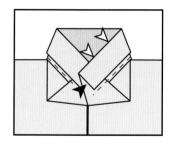

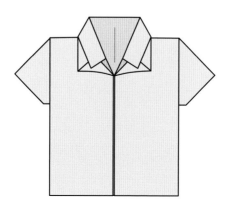

HIGH-HEEL SHOE

High-heel Shoe

All bills are suitable, although only the numeral denomination of the dollar will be displayed on the final model (see examples) and only when the front of the bill is used for the shoe's toe section. You will need a pair of tweezers and two paper clips. Double-stick tape is handy but optional. Paper substitutions: The Shoe displays both sides of the paper.

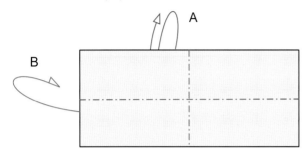

1. Begin with the side intended as the toe section up.
Note: With bill positioned upright, top left corner design on dollar will appear on toe section. To have top right corner design on toe section instead, rotate your bill 180 degrees. Desired design is now on left and bill is upside down.

A. Mtn. fold in half lengthwise; unfold.
B. Mtn. fold in half.

2. Fold edge to edge; unfold.

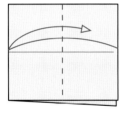

3. Fold edge to crease; unfold.

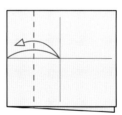

4. Fold corners of top flap to center.

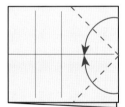

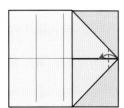

5. Fold pt. in on border line behind.
Note: This fold determines length of heel spike.

6. Fold edges to center.

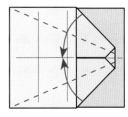

7.
A. Unfold flap from behind.
B. Fold edges to center.
Crease only as shown.
Unfold.

8.
A. Fold edges in on border line
or 1/4 distance to center.
B. Fold flap over on crease.

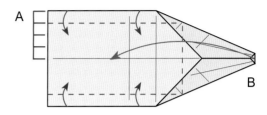

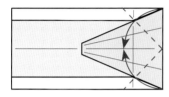

9. Evenly fold corners to center.

10. Fold edges to 1/8-inch
distance from center line.

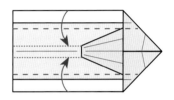

11. On both sides:
A. Mtn. fold section in half.
Crease only as shown. Unfold.
B. Unfold flap.

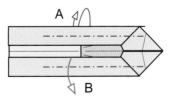

Turn model over.

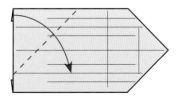

12. Fold edge down to crease.
*Note: If you chose the right corner design
in step 1, fold edge up to opposite crease.
(See 12a.)*

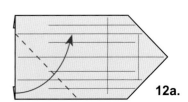

12a.

E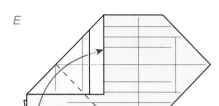

13. Fold edge to edge under top flap.
Note: If you chose the right corner design, mirror instructions. (See 13a.)

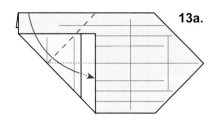

13a.

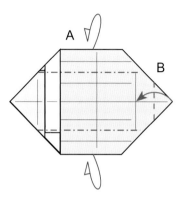

14.
A. Mtn. fold edges behind on creases.
B. Fold pt. to crease.

15.
A. Mtn. fold toe section in half; unfold.
B. Fold section over on edge; unfold.

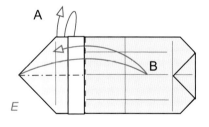

16.
1. Push on sides to open layers, raising center line.
2. Use tweezers to start fold. Bend midpt. of edge in.
3. Push to fold edges in between pts.

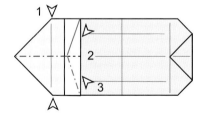

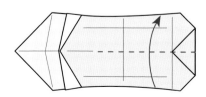

17. Fold sides of heel and midsection together.

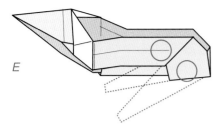

E

18. Pull heel out to position outlined in red. Pinch as shown to hold layers in place as you pull heel farther out to position outlined in blue. Reset side folds.

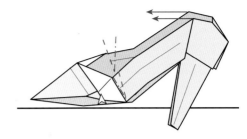

19. Place toe of shoe on flat surface. Push on sides to open toe section. Bring rest of shoe forward on creases and heel in line on surface. Pleats are created in the process on both sides. Pinch pleats flat. Use paper clips to set.

20.
A. Lightly pinch edges of toe to define.
B. Round top of heel.
C. Push on edges of spike to round on creases.

Optional: Place double-stick tape under toe of shoe. Adhere to a slip of paper, card, etc.

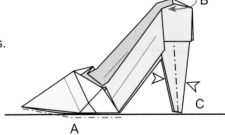

21.
A. Round sides out on creases, slightly bending edges in.
B. Use a tweezer to redefine folds and edges, lift layers, and mold model.
C. Push on center of left edge to create instep of right shoe or vice versa.

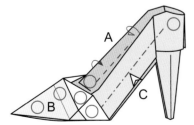

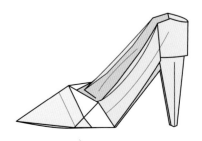

CHRISTMAS TREE

Christmas Tree

For the greenest Christmas tree, use the back of any bill. The star is mainly created from the side border on the front of the bill. Avoid bills with overly thin side front borders. Paper substitutions: The Christmas Tree displays both sides of the paper. The tree displays one side and the star, the other.

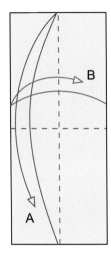

1. Begin with the desired side down.
Place the star end on top.
A. Fold in half; unfold.
B. Fold in half lengthwise; unfold.

Turn model over.

2.
A. Fold edge to crease; unfold.
B. Fold corner to edge; unfold.
Repeat.

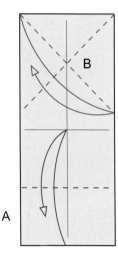

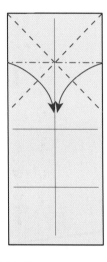

3. Fold sides in on creases.
Align all edges. Set folds.

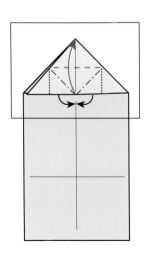

4. Mtn. fold each flap in half; unfold.
Fold midpt. of edge to pt.
Fold edges to center.
Flatten to set folds.

5. On each side:
Fold corner pt. of flap up.
Push on edge to flatten
section on creases.

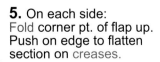

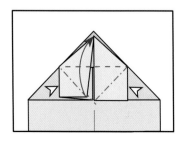

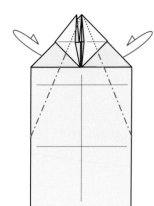

6. Turn model over.
Fold edges to center.

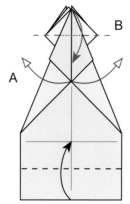

7.
A. Unfold flaps.
B. Fold pt. of top flap down.
C. Fold edge to crease.

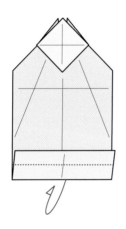

8. Turn model over and fold edge only to crease.

9. On each side:
Open and lift layer. Fold layer up on crease just enough to align pt. of flap on crease. Flatten to set all folds.

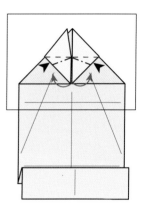

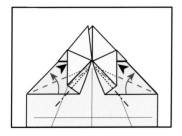

10. On each side:
Open layer. Lift pt. to fold edge to edge as far up as possible. Realign pt. on side of crease. Flatten to set remaining folds.

11. Rabbit ear fold each flap:
1. Pinch fold flap in half, folding sides to align with edge.
2. **Fold** new flap outward and down.

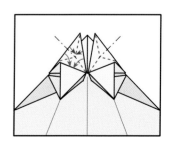

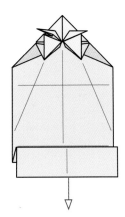

12. Unfold flap. **Turn model over.**

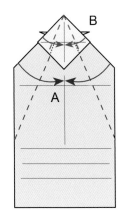

13.
A. Fold edges in on creases. Fold is made partially beneath top layer.
B. Fold edges to center. Do not fold side flaps of star.

Note: Front view is depicted for reference only.

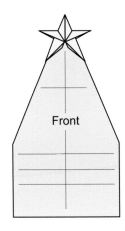

Front

14. Lightly fold edge to crease. *Note: Redefine top crease if needed.* Firmly set section only.

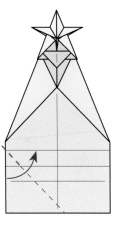

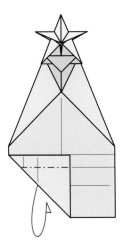

15. Keep flap aligned. Mtn. fold section behind. Crease as shown. Unfold flap completely.

Repeat steps 14 and 15 on right.

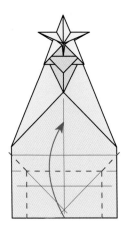

16. Fold edges in on creases, as you fold section up on crease. Flatten to set folds.

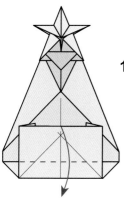

17. Fold flap down on crease.

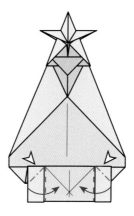

18. On each side:
Fold edges in. Push to flatten overlapping section symmetrically.

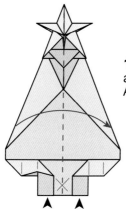

19. Fold model in half. Open sides at a wide angle, forming a triangular base at bottom end. Adjust base flaps if necessary to stand tree.

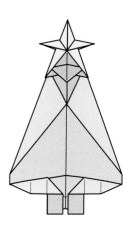

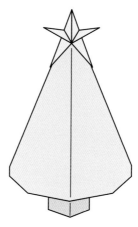

ROSE

Rose

Use the back of a one-dollar bill or any larger-denomination bill with the old design. You will need tape and a pair of tweezers to form and shape your rose. Paper substitutions: The Rose displays one side of the paper.

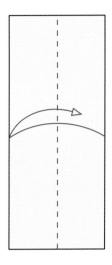

1. Begin with the desired side down. Fold in half; unfold.

2. Fold edges to center.

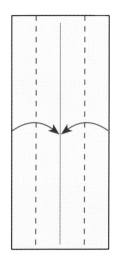

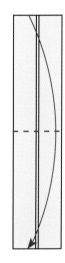

3. Fold in half.

4. Evenly fold corners to center.

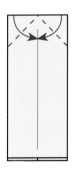

E

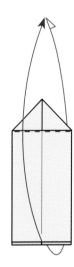

5. Fold section up along edges. Mtn. fold section behind up. Match sides.

Unfold steps 5, 4, and 3.

Note: Side with flaps is up.

6. On both sides: Mtn. fold crease into edge. Fold new edge to center. Crease only as shown. **Unfold.**

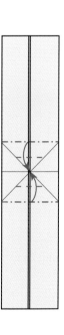

7. Fold edges to center Crease only as shown.

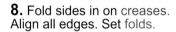

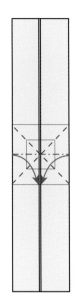

8. Fold sides in on creases. Align all edges. Set folds.

9. Flatten tip on creases:
1. Lift section perpendicular on crease.
2. Align edges. Stretch open sides. Flatten point on creases. (See 9a.)

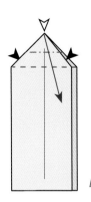

9a.

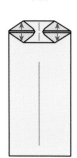

Rotate model as shown.

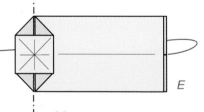

10. Mtn. fold open flap.

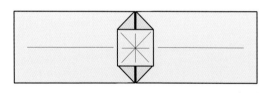

11. Turn model over.

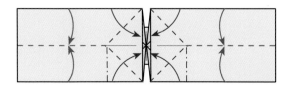

12. Rabbit ear fold each side:
1. Fold each edge to center. Crease only as shown. Unfold.
2. Fold edges up as you fold sides together.
3. Fold new flap down and flatten to set folds.

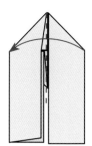

13. Fold flap over.

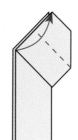

14. Fold pt. to pt.

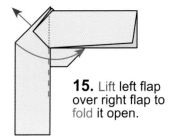

15. Lift left flap over right flap to fold it open.

16. Fold pt. to pt.

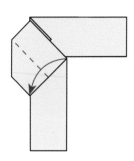

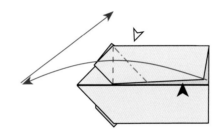

17. Squash fold flap:
1. Fold flap to left, then lift perpendicular.
2. Open layers.
3. Push to flatten section symmetrically.
Note: Align diagonal folds with edges beneath.

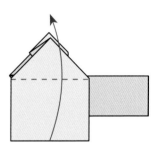

18. Fold flap up. Make fold in line with edges beneath.

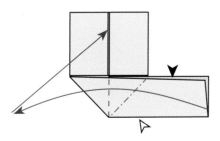

19. Squash fold flap.
(See step 17.)
Repeat step 18.

20. Rabbit ear fold each side:
1. Fold each edge to center.
Crease only as shown. Unfold.
2. Fold edges up as you fold sides together.
3. **Fold** new flap to side indicated by **mtn. fold**.

E

21. Fold flap down.

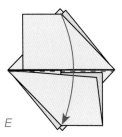

E

22. Fold edge up as shown.

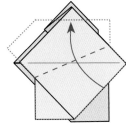

23. Lift flap over top layer. Rotate model 180 degrees. Repeat steps 21 and 22.

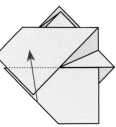

24. Match center edges as shown. Tape sides together. Fold edge in line with edge beneath.

Turn model over.

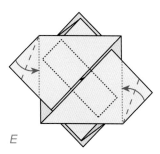

E

25. Push edge flat to fold pt. to pt. Pinch to round edge up.

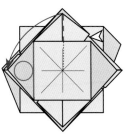

26. Hold corner of bottom layer. Pinch end of flap with tweezers. Twist tightly toward center.

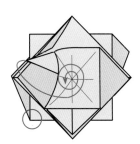

27.
A. Pinch straight edges with tweezers and twist to pleat.
B. Use tweezers to curl all petals.

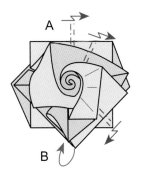

A

B

STATUE OF LIBERTY

Statue of Liberty

The Statue of Liberty requires two one-dollar bills. Ideally, the bill used to create the statue's arms, book, and torch should have even top and bottom borders on both sides of the bill. Paper substitutions: The Statue of Liberty displays both sides of the paper. The book and torch display the opposite side of the paper from the rest of the model.

1. Begin with design of pyramid on top end and desired side down.
A. Fold in half; unfold.
B. Mtn. fold in half.

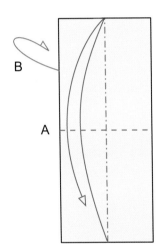

2. Fold sides in half. Unfold completely. Place desired side down.

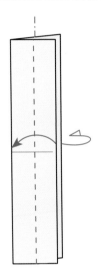

3. Fold each side edge to center line to establish creases. Unfold. Fold sides in on creases. Align all edges. Set folds.

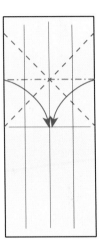

4. Mtn. fold pt. in line with crease behind.

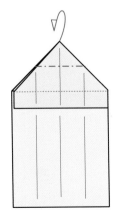

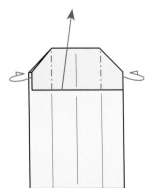

5. Lift flap up, folding sides in on creases to center.

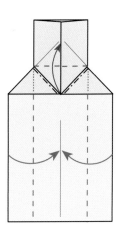

6. On each side:
Fold pt. up, while folding sides in on creases and **mtn. folding** along edges.

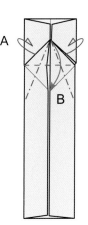

A

B

7.
A. Mtn. fold edges behind to center. Match sides. **Unfold.**
B. Fold flaps down.

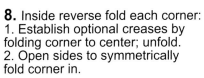

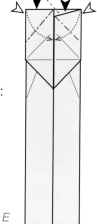

8. Inside reverse fold each corner:
1. Establish optional creases by folding corner to center; unfold.
2. Open sides to symmetrically fold corner in.

E

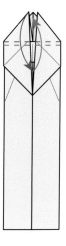

9. Fold flaps down. Fold back up below original pt.

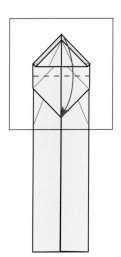

10. Fold section in half.

Rotate model as shown.

11. On both sides:
Fold edge to center. Push to flatten overlapping section.

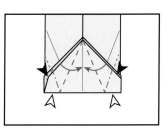

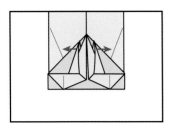

12. Evenly pull flaps out to side. Make pts. and match sides. Flatten to set.

13. Fold sections down from behind.

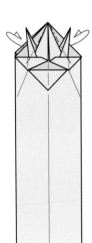

14. Mtn. fold edges behind. Do not fold spikes or back layer.

15. Temporarily place model aside. Using second bill, begin with the desired side up.
A. Mtn. fold edges behind on border lines.
B. Fold in half.

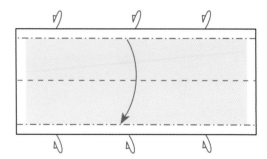

16. Fold sides in half. **Unfold completely.** Place back of bill up and bill upright.

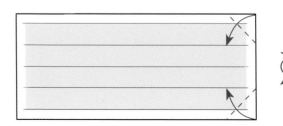

17. Fold corners to creases. **Turn model over.**

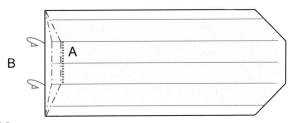

18.
A. Use triple-line design as guide. Crease as shown, starting with middle fold. Extend mtn. fold to corners. **Unfold.**
B. Mtn. fold on border line as shown, starting with middle fold. Extend fold to corners.

19. Refold edges in on border lines. Refold sides to center.

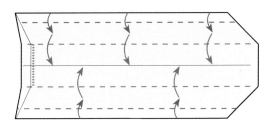

Note: Only folded sections of borders are depicted in white.

20. Turn model over.

21. Fold each edge between corner pt. and pt. determined by edge beneath. **Unfold.**

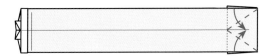

22. Slip second bill under head section of first bill as shown. Chin is positioned between letters *N* and *E.* Use a bulldog clip where indicated to hold bill in place. Fold edge in on crease on layer beneath.

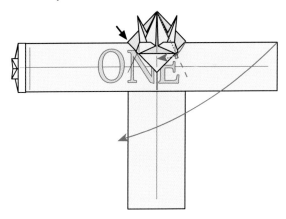

23. Fold flap up against edge of flap. Crease as shown.

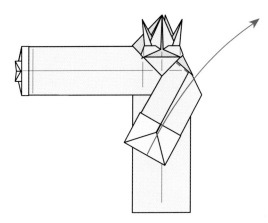

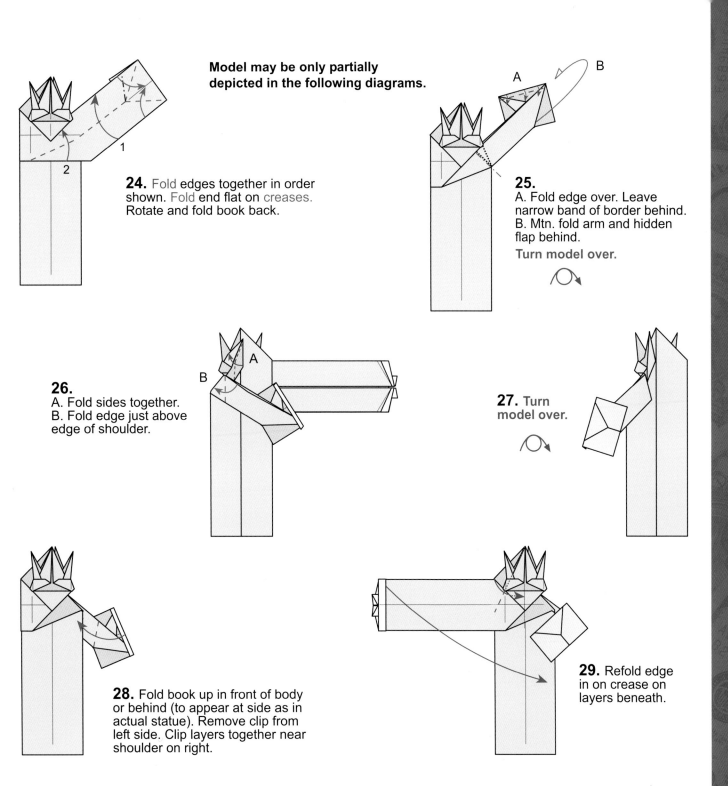

Model may be only partially depicted in the following diagrams.

24. Fold edges together in order shown. Fold end flat on creases. Rotate and fold book back.

25.
A. Fold edge over. Leave narrow band of border behind.
B. Mtn. fold arm and hidden flap behind.

Turn model over.

26.
A. Fold sides together.
B. Fold edge just above edge of shoulder.

27. Turn model over.

28. Fold book up in front of body or behind (to appear at side as in actual statue). Remove clip from left side. Clip layers together near shoulder on right.

29. Refold edge in on crease on layers beneath.

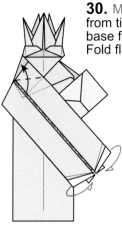

30. Mtn. fold flap in half from tip to base. Extend base fold to outlined pt. Fold flap up.

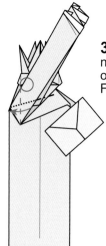

31. Pinch left side of flap near base. Fold entire arm over, folding edge to edge. Flatten overlapping section.

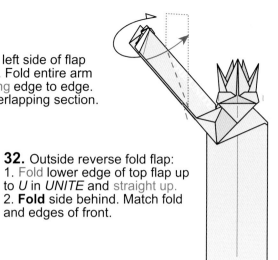

32. Outside reverse fold flap:
1. Fold lower edge of top flap up to *U* in *UNITE* and straight up.
2. **Fold** side behind. Match fold and edges of front.

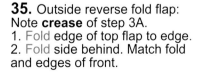

33. Unfold top flap.

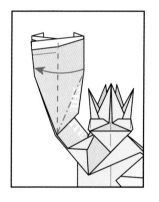

34. Refold flap on outside. Align folds and edges with those beneath. Repeat steps 32 and 33 on flap behind.

35. Outside reverse fold flap: Note **crease** of step 3A.
1. Fold edge of top flap to edge.
2. Fold side behind. Match fold and edges of front.

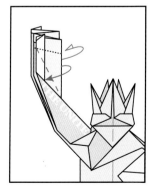

36. Fold upper arm back and perpendicular on crease.

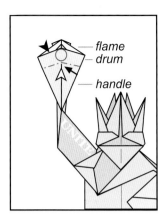

flame
drum
handle

37. *Note: Indicated split should end just below* crease *of step 3A. Adjust if needed.*
Open layers to pinch drum near center.
Push under crease to define edge of drum.
Pinch length of edge with tweezers to set.

38.
A. Pinch sides of handle and flames together.
Push in and up to shape and round drum.
B. Lift and align border flaps behind flame.
Fold over corners of flaps together twice to lock sides.

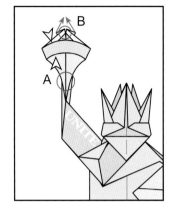

39.
A. Push to round pt. back and edge under. (Result shown in last diagram.)
B. Rabbit ear fold flap by pinching flap in half down to base.

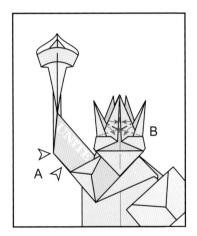

40.
A. Fold side spikes down then up at angle.
B. Fold pt. of chin under.

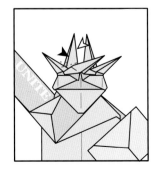

41. On each of back spikes: Open sides to inside reverse fold flap in.

Square Box

You will need two square sheets of paper to create a box with a lid. Ideally, one sheet should be 1/4-inch square smaller. Trim adjacent sides as shown. Fold the bottom of the box from the smaller sheet and the lid from the larger sheet. Two lid designs are presented in the instructions.

Use a square box folded from a 6-inch square sheet of paper to present the Lucky Frog, Teddy Bear, Four-leaf Clover, Flower (smaller), or several Roses. The Turtle and larger Flower require a square box folded from two 7-inch square sheets.

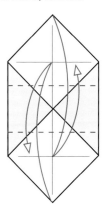

Trim 1/4 inch off adjacent sides.

1. Start with the smaller sheet.
Begin with desired side down.
A. Fold in half; unfold.
B. Mtn. fold in half; unfold. Repeat.

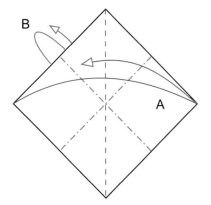

2. Fold all pts. to center.
Unfold top and bottom flaps.

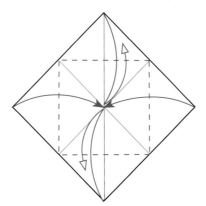

3. Fold each pt. to crease; unfold.

4. Fold edges to center.

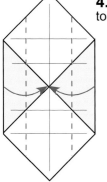

5. Mtn. fold each pt. behind to crease.

6.
A. Lift sides perpendicular.
B. On each end:
Fold edges up to creases, lifting side on crease and forming both corners.

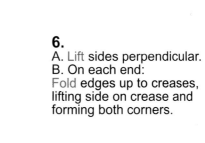

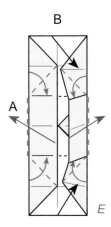

7. Fold sides in on creases. Unfold flap to line bottom of box.

E

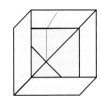

Repeat the instructions, using the larger sheet, to fold a box cover of similar dimensions.

Proceed with the following instructions to create a shallower box lid.

Complete steps 1 through 4 of prior instructions.

5.
A. Unfold sides.
B. Fold pts. to creases.

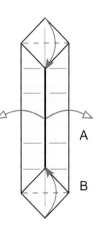

A

B

6. Fold edges to center; unfold.

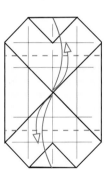

7. On both sides: Fold edge to crease. Refold new edge in on crease.

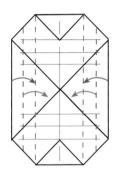

B

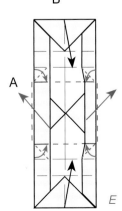

A

E

8.
A. Lift sides perpendicular.
B. On each end: Fold edges up to creases, lifting side on crease and forming both corners.

9. Fold sides in on creases.

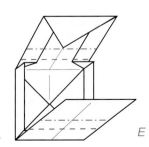

E

RING BOX

Ring Box

The Ring Box has two parts, the box and an insert that holds and displays the ring. It requires two sheets of paper, approximately 6 inches square each such as origami paper.

The Box

1. Begin with desired side down. Fold in half; unfold. Repeat.

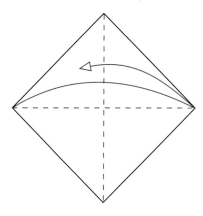

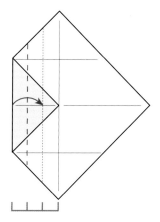

2.
A. Fold pt. to center.
B. Mtn. fold pts. to center; unfold.

3. Hold flap in place. Fold edge in to 1/3 distance of center line.

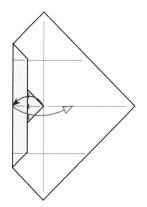

4. Width of flaps should be equal. Fold smaller flap over to check. Adjust if needed. Unfold layers.

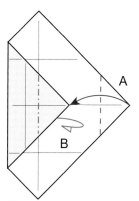

5.
A. Fold pt. to pt.
B. Mtn. fold end of flap under on crease.

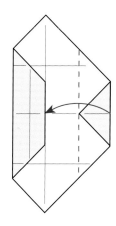

6. Fold edge to center.

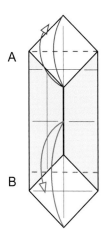

A

B

7. Complete A and B on each end.
A. Fold top pt. to *V* pt. Unfold.
B. Fold bottom pt. to center to redirect creases on top layers. Unfold.

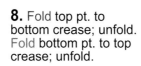

8. Fold top pt. to bottom crease; unfold. Fold bottom pt. to top crease; unfold.

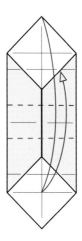

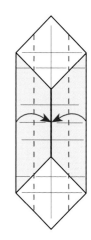

9. Fold sides to center.

10. Mtn. fold model in half. Lift as indicated to fold edge to new edge, forming corner in the process. Repeat to form remaining corners.

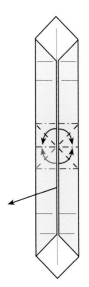

E

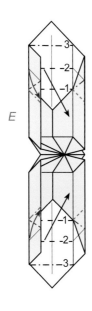

11. On each end:
Fold edges up to creases, forming both corners and lifting end on crease 1.
Fold flap in on crease 2.
Mtn. fold 3 is made in the process, forming flap to line part of box bottom.

12. Pinch center edge flat to raise lid. Use box as is or fold and place insert in box to hold and display ring. Box is meant to be an open box.
Optional: Use a sticker or tie with ribbon to close box.

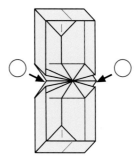

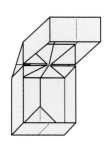

The Insert

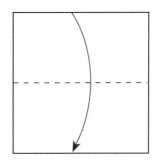

1. Begin with the desired side down. Fold in half.

2. Fold edges 1/4 inch from edge. Repeat behind.

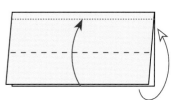

3. Fold edge over flaps.

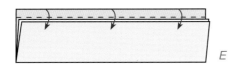

E

4. Fold edges 1/4 inch from edge.

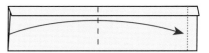

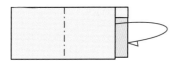

5. Mtn. fold flap in half.

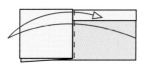

6. Fold side over along edge. Unfold. **Turn model over.**

7. Mtn. fold crease in to edge. Fold new edge to edge.

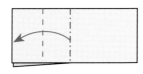

8. Unfold flap.

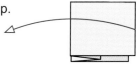

9.
A. Fold edge to crease.
B. Pull to unfold flap.

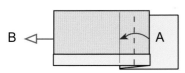

10.
A. Fold each edge to crease.
Crease as shown. Unfold.
B. Fold edge to edge.
Crease as shown. Unfold.

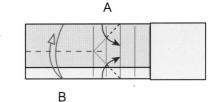

11. Fold each edge to center while refolding edges to crease. **Fold** flap over. Flatten to set folds.

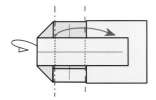

12. Mtn. fold section behind on crease. **Fold** new edge over on crease without folding top flap.

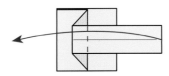

13. Fold flap over on crease.

Rotate model as shown.
14. Lift flap perpendicular and round as desired. Thread through ring. Fold end under square.

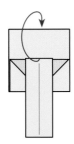

Place insert in box.

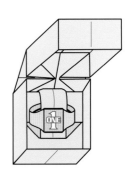